The BP Oil Spill

Cuyahoga Falls
Library
Cuyahoga Falls, Ohio

PETER BENOIT

Children's Press®
An Imprint of Scholastic Inc.
New York Toronto London Auckland Sydney
Mexico City New Delhi Hong Kong
Danbury, Connecticut

Content Consultant
W. Scott Pegau, PhD
Prince William Sound Science Center
Cordova, Alaska

Library of Congress Cataloging-in-Publication Data

Benoit, Peter, 1955–
  The BP oil spill/Peter Benoit.
     p. cm.—(A true book)
  Includes bibliographical references and index.
  ISBN-13: 978-0-531-20630-0 (lib. bdg.)   ISBN-13: 978-0-531-28999-0 (pbk.)
  ISBN-10: 0-531-20630-0 (lib. bdg.)   ISBN-10: 0-531-28999-0 (pbk.)
  1. BP Deepwater Horizon Explosion and Oil Spill, 2010—Juvenile literature. 2. Oil spills—Mexico,
Gulf of—History—21st century—Juvenile literature. 3. Oil spills—Environmental aspects—
Mexico, Gulf of—History—21st century—Juvenile literature. 4. Oil wells—Mexico, Gulf of—
Blowouts—History—21st century—Juvenile literature. 5. BP (Firm)—Juvenile literature. I. Title.
II. Series.

  TD427.P4B45 2011
  363.738'20916364—dc22   2010045927

All rights reserved. Published in 2011 by Children's Press, an imprint of Scholastic Inc.
Printed in China. 62
SCHOLASTIC, CHILDREN'S PRESS, A TRUE BOOK and associated logos are trademarks and/or
registered trademarks of Scholastic Inc.

1 2 3 4 5 6 7 8 9 10 R 18 17 16 15 14 13 12 11

Find the Truth!

Everything you are about to read is true *except* for one of the sentences on this page.

Which one is **TRUE**?

T or F   No one survived the Deepwater Horizon explosion.

T or F   The BP oil spill affected more than 8,000 species.

Find the answers in this book.

BEACH CLOSED

Contents

THE **BIG** TRUTH!

Animals in Danger

Rescued sea turtle

Oil found onshore

More than 33,000 workers and 6,300 boats helped clean up the oil spill.

A U.S. Coast Guard crew pulls in a skimmer.

Coast Guard firefighting boats tried to put out the flames on Deepwater Horizon with powerful streams of water.

CHAPTER 1

Trouble in the Gulf

At 9:45 p.m. on April 20, 2010, an **oil rig** called the Deepwater Horizon exploded and caught fire. The rig had been drilling for oil deep under the ocean floor in the Gulf of Mexico, some 41 miles (66 kilometers) off the Louisiana coast. Seventeen of the 98 workers on the rig were injured in the explosion. Eleven went missing. Meanwhile, the oil well the rig had been drilling was left uncapped. Oil began leaking into the ocean.

Deepwater Horizon cost $350 million to build in 2001.

Firefighters were unable to control the intense fire. Witnesses watched the smoke and flames from as far as 35 miles (56 km) away. Deepwater Horizon burned for just over 36 hours. Then, on the morning of April 22, it sank to the seafloor nearly 5,000 feet (1,500 meters) below. The search for the missing workers went on for hours as another disaster brewed beneath the water.

Rescue workers used helicopters to transport injured people to hospitals.

The column of smoke from the burning rig could be seen from space.

A gigantic cloud of smoke towered above the burning oil rig.

Less than two days after Deepwater Horizon went down, the U.S. Coast Guard found an **oil slick** 5 miles (8 km) long. Investigators discovered the uncapped well was gushing thousands of barrels of oil per day into the Gulf of Mexico. By the time the well was capped, the Deepwater Horizon accident had caused the largest oil spill ever in U.S. waters.

Specially stabilized offshore rigs like the Deepwater Horizon are designed to drill more than 5,000 feet (1,500 m) below the water's surface.

CHAPTER 2

Deep-Water Disaster

The Deepwater Horizon was leased by BP, an energy company. At 396 feet (121 m) long and 256 feet (78 m) wide, the rig could drill 30,000 feet (9,100 m) into the earth. In 2009, it set the record for drilling the deepest underwater well.

But Deepwater Horizon also had problems. The Coast Guard had investigated several fires. After one accident in 2008, the rig even began to tip over.

 Oil products include gasoline, jet fuel, and plastic.

Oil rig workers are responsible for keeping drilling bits and other equipment in good condition.

Trouble Down Below

Friction from oil drilling makes the machinery and the super-hard tip of the drill, called the bit, very hot. Workers cool the bit with a substance known as drilling mud. Drilling mud is made of clay, water, and small amounts of chemicals. It helps keep pressure on the hole so gases do not leak out during drilling. Drilling mud is backed up by a blowout preventer, or BOP.

A BOP is a device that checks for dangerous changes in pressure around the drill. A blowout is an uncontrolled release of gas or fluid pressure. It is one of the biggest dangers faced by oil workers. In late March 2010, workers noticed damage to the Deepwater Horizon BOP. It had been leaking fluids at least three different times. These fluid leaks can prevent the BOP from working properly, but BP decided to keep using it anyway.

The blowout preventer is one of the most important pieces of equipment on an oil rig.

A blowout used to be called a gusher.

Under Pressure

A decision was made to abandon the well and come back for the oil later. This is a common practice for oil drillers. Hours before the explosion, a BP official ordered the chief driller to replace the drilling mud with seawater to begin sealing up the well. The chief driller argued that it was unsafe. But afraid of being fired, he followed the order.

Working on an oil rig is physically demanding.

Some types of oil workers are called roughnecks.

An oil rig's operating cost includes salaries for its large crew.

Speed

The next step was to plug the well with cement. It cost $750,000 per day to operate the Deepwater Horizon, and BP's work was behind schedule. The company needed to work fast to keep down costs. They did not take the time to make sure the cement had dried properly.

The Accident

On the night of the accident, the Deepwater Horizon crew reported a loud hissing noise. A bubble of **flammable** gas had flown up the tube that surrounded the drill. As it rose, seals meant to keep gases under control burst apart. An explosion rocked the rig. Alarms blared, and workers ran for the lifeboats. They had less than five minutes to escape before fire roared through the Deepwater Horizon.

The Deepwater Horizon crew members had little time to reach lifeboats and escape the blaze.

A company called Transocean owned the Deepwater Horizon.

Exxon Valdez

Another gigantic oil spill happened on March 24, 1989, in Prince William Sound, Alaska. That day, the tanker ship *Exxon Valdez* struck an underwater reef and began gushing oil. By the time it stopped, at least 11 million gallons (41.6 million L) of oil had leaked from the ship. The disaster damaged fishing grounds and killed thousands of animals including seabirds, seals, and orcas.

The effects of the *Exxon Valdez* oil spill are still being felt today in Prince William Sound.

Ships and oil rigs were brought in to try to recover the Deepwater Horizon's spilled oil.

CHAPTER 3

From Bad to Worse

The oil slick was discovered on the afternoon of April 22, though the leak may have started a day earlier. On April 24, the U.S. Coast Guard and BP agreed the well was leaking 1,000 barrels (42,000 gallons/159,000 L) of oil per day. Other experts, however, claimed it had to be more. Soon, the Coast Guard's number climbed to 5,000 barrels (210,000 gallons/795,000 L) per day.

Dozens of vessels helped contain the spill.

The Oil Spreads

A weather system with strong winds from the south blew the oil patch far from the leak site. By April 25, it covered 580 square miles (1,500 sq km). Just five days later, it had grown into a slick almost seven times as large. Television and Internet viewers worldwide watched underwater cameras that showed the black oil gushing into the Gulf of Mexico.

This map shows the site of the Deep Horizon oil rig and the extent of the oil spill after the explosion.

Breton became a wildlife refuge in 1904.

Cleanup workers set up barriers around Breton National Wildlife Refuge to keep oil out.

As the oil spread, it moved closer to land, where it would affect life along the coast. By early May, the spill threatened the Breton National Wildlife Refuge in Louisiana. This is home to brown pelicans, piping plovers, and many other bird species. The slick also inched toward the Gulf Stream, a powerful ocean **current**. If the oil reached the Gulf Stream, the current could carry it up the East Coast of the United States.

Beautiful beaches were spoiled by oily lumps of tar that washed up along the shore.

Oil Strikes Land

The first week of June, oil washed onto the Louisiana coast and the outer islands of Mississippi and Alabama. On June 23, lumps of oil called tar balls darkened the white sand beaches in Pensacola, Florida. More tar balls appeared at Galveston, Texas, on the other end of the Gulf, in early July.

Fixing the Leak

Drilling began on May 2 on a relief well that would intersect with the leaking well. Meanwhile, BP tried to slow the leak. At first, nothing really worked. Then, on July 12, a cap was added to the broken BOP. Oil flow stopped three days later. Finally, in September, a working BOP was installed on the well. On September 17, cement was pumped into the well through the completed relief well and the leak was permanently sealed.

Robots were used to help repair leaking pipes underwater.

The leaking oil formed massive clouds underwater.

23

Animals in Danger

The BP oil spill hit Gulf shore **ecosystems** hard. An ecosystem is a community of life-forms and the land and sea conditions surrounding that community. Life-forms include plants, animals, fungi, and other living things. Ecosystems affected by the spill included those on beaches, the ocean floor, and marshes near the shore. In all, the oil affected thousands of species including sea turtles, seabirds, many kinds of fish, and a variety of reptiles and mammals.

Brown Pelicans

Brown pelicans soaked in oil overheat because they cannot stay cool. Oil also gets into their eggs and kills their chicks.

Shrimps

Oil absorbed by crustacean species such as shrimps not only harmed the shrimps but could poison shrimp eaters such as birds—and people.

Sea Turtles

Volunteers moved sea turtle eggs away from oily beaches so the baby turtles had a chance to swim safely in clean water.

Tourists spend about $34 billion per year visiting the Gulf Coast.

BEACH CLOSED

The beaches of Grand Isle are normally filled with tourists, not cleanup workers.

Human Costs

The spill also hurt thousands of Gulf state workers. Tourists concerned about the oil canceled plans to visit the Gulf shore. At Grand Isle, Louisiana, for example, fears about the spill reduced the usual summer crowd from 10,000 visitors to 100. Tourist communities worried that people who went on vacation elsewhere in 2010 might never come back to the Gulf.

Industries that depend on the sea were also severely damaged. The oil spoiled many good fishing areas. Sports fishing—catching wild fish such as shark and tuna for fun—was ruined for the year. The commercial fishers who catch shrimp and snapper for Americans' dinner tables lost a lot of money. It cost shoppers around the country, too. Prices of shrimps, oysters, and other Gulf seafood rose everywhere.

Fishing boats remained docked as oil spread through the Gulf of Mexico.

After booms were placed, skimmers were used to skim oil from the water.

CHAPTER 4

Cleanup

Workers hired to clean up the mess tackled the job on three fronts. First, they tried to keep surface oil away from sensitive ecosystems. They used floating barriers called **booms** to block the movement of oil. Problems arose, though, when waves carried oil over and under the booms.

Many methods used to clean up oil in the Gulf were the same as those for the *Exxon Valdez* spill.

Dispersing the Oil

Second, the cleanup workers hoped to **disperse** the oil by adding special chemicals to the water. If the slicks could be broken into tiny drops, it would be easier for bacteria in the water to dissolve the oil. Not only did workers apply chemicals to the surface, they also used the substance in deep water.

Airplanes spread dispersing chemicals onto the oil slicks.

Workers used almost 2 million gallons (7.6 million L) of dispersing chemicals.

Large gatherings of phytoplankton can cause water to appear green.

As the oil breaks down and dissolves, it makes the water toxic. This affected the Gulf ecosystem by killing tiny floating plants called **phytoplankton**. All sea life depends on phytoplankton. Tiny animals eat it. They are in turn eaten by larger animals, which are eaten by even larger animals, and so on.

Removing the Oil

Workers removed oil from the water. Booms corralled oil into areas where machines called skimmers scooped it up. Cleanup crews use several types of skimmers. Drum, disk, and rope skimmers attract oil as they are pulled along. The oil sticks to the skimmers. It is then wiped off and stored in collection containers. Another kind of skimmer sucks in water and oil like a vacuum.

The Tools of Removal

In places far from sensitive areas such as wildlife reserves, workers burned the oil. This is the fastest and simplest way to remove oil from the water. But burning causes air pollution. Plus, the oil that is left still has to be skimmed off the water.

Oil-eating bacteria also helped with cleanup. Tiny bacteria live everywhere. They live on the ocean floor, in trees, and inside the human body. A few of the millions of bacteria species living in the ocean eat oil. They helped dissolve the spilled oil, but they could not do all the work by themselves.

The controlled burns for the BP oil spill were the biggest ever.

33

Bacteria at Work

The oil in the Gulf doesn't all come from spills. Every year, thousands of gallons of oil escape the seafloor on their own. Some Gulf bacteria live on it. Scientists think bacteria that were already in the water ate part of the oil plumes from the BP disaster. Unfortunately, as these bacteria multiply, they use up more oxygen in the water. If the oxygen level gets too low, other species die.

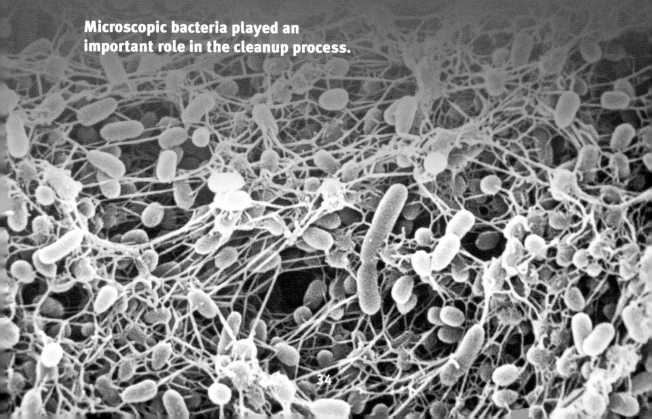

Microscopic bacteria played an important role in the cleanup process.

Cost of Cleanup

The cleanup process caused problems of its own. Several of the dispersing chemicals, for example, cause cancer. In addition, doctors reported cases of workers and people onshore suffering from breathing problems, skin rashes, and nausea. The crisis also led to stress and other problems. Cleanup workers faced dangers and many people onshore lost jobs and money.

Oil can cause health problems through contact with the skin or when workers breathe in oil fumes.

Workers wore special clothing to help protect against sickness caused by oil.

The oil well was finally capped after months of work.

CHAPTER 5

After the Spill

An estimated 205.8 million gallons (779 million L) of oil escaped before crews capped the well. Offshore, massive underwater oil **plumes** 4,000 feet (1,200 m) below the surface cannot **evaporate**. It will take a long time for them to dissolve and mix in with the surrounding water. This is because deep water is denser than water near the surface. Oil-eating bacteria living in the ocean will do a lot to help this process.

 Workers permanently sealed the well on September 17, 2010.

Endangered Again

Animal species that had been **endangered** before the spill faced renewed threats to their survival after the spill. Some experts believe that more than 20 percent of the Gulf's endangered Atlantic bluefin tuna may have died. The brown pelican, meanwhile, had just escaped the endangered species list for the first time in decades. But oil killed so many of the birds that it could end up threatened once more.

Timeline of the Oil Spill

April 20, 2010

An explosion on the Deepwater Horizon leads to a deadly fire.

April 22

An oil slick is discovered in the Gulf of Mexico.

West Indian manatees swim to Gulf waters every summer. Now oil may get into their bodies when they eat sea plants. Dozens of Kemp's ridley sea turtles, already the world's rarest sea turtle species, washed up dead after the spill. Volunteers tried to save the turtles' young by putting eggs in machines to keep them warm. The spill's effects on some species may not show up for years. Altogether, more than 8,000 species were affected.

May 6
Oil hits the Louisiana coast more than 40 miles (64 km) from the spill site.

July 15
The leaking well is capped and the well temporarily closed.

September 17
The well is permanently sealed with cement.

BP is the world's fourth-largest company.

Tony Hayward resigned from BP in July 2010.

Hard-Hit Company

The spill damaged BP's image. The disaster itself created plenty of bad feelings. And then BP denied the leak was as severe as it turned out to be. Tony Hayward, the company's top official, did more harm by complaining that the spill took up all his time.

The financial cost to the company has also been high. In 2010, BP spent more than $10 billion on the cleanup.

Even before the well was capped, BP faced legal cases filed by hundreds of companies and individuals. BP spent millions of dollars settling with others to avoid future legal action. Profits took a hit as well. The company's value fell by more than half during the disaster. In September 2010, BP predicted that the spill's total cost to them would likely be about $32 billion.

Many people around the world protested against BP.

41

Costly Decisions

Decisions made in order to save time and money on the Deepwater Horizon ended up having great costs. For 11 people aboard the rig, the price was their lives. Thousands more lost their jobs. It will take several more years to understand the full impact of the spill and the real effectiveness of cleanup efforts. Researchers are still studying the causes that led to the spill. ★

Even with the oil well capped, the U.S. government continues to collect oil and water samples to help them predict where the oil will go next.

Oil from the spill could continue to cause problems for years to come.

42

True Statistics

Amount of oil spilled in BP disaster: 205.8 million gal. (779 million L)

Number of people on Deepwater Horizon when it exploded: 126

Number of people killed in the explosion: 11

Cost to build Deepwater Horizon in 2001: $350 million

Amount of time that oil leaked from the uncapped well: about 3 months

Maximum amount of oil leaked per day: 5,000 barrels

Length of oil plume found near wellhead: 22 mi. (35 km) long

Amount of oil-dispersing chemicals used: Almost 2 million gal. (7.6 million L)

Thickness of oil on Gulf seafloor: 2 inches (5 cm)

Did you find the truth?

(F) No one survived the Deepwater Horizon explosion.

(T) The BP oil spill affected more than 8,000 species.

Resources

Books

Chapman, Garry, and Gary Hodges. *Oil*. Mankato, MN: Smart Apple, 2011.

Chiang, Mona, Cody Crane, Karina Hamalainen, and Lynda Jones. *Oil Spill: Disaster in the Gulf*. New York: Scholastic, 2010.

Farndon, John. *Oil*. New York: DK, 2007.

Manatt, Kathleen. *Searching for Oil*. Ann Arbor, MI: Cherry Lake, 2008.

Parks, Peggy. *Oil Spills*. Detroit: KidHaven Press, 2005.

Powell, Jillian. *Oil Spills*. Mankato, MN: Bridgestone Books, 2003.

Streissguth, Thomas. *The Exxon Valdez*. Mankato, MN: Capstone High-Interest Books, 2003.

Thomas, William David. *Oil Rig Worker*. New York: Marshall Cavendish Benchmark, 2010.

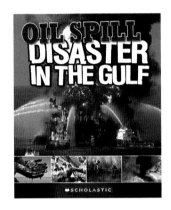

Organizations and Web Sites

National Geographic: Gulf Oil Spill News and Pictures
http://news.nationalgeographic.com/news/gulf-oil-spill-news/
Read articles and check out pictures of the spill.

National Wildlife Federation: The Big Oil Spill
www.nwf.org/Kids/Ranger-Rick/People-and-Places/Ranger-Rick-on-the-Big-Oil-Spill.aspx
Explore the details and study maps of the BP oil spill.

Our Amazing Planet: Gulf Oil Spill—Animals at Risk
www.ouramazingplanet.com/gulf-oil-spill-animals-at-risk-0255/
Watch a slide show about the animals affected by the oil spill.

Places to Visit

Breton National Wildlife Refuge
U.S. Fish and Wildlife Service
Southeast Louisiana Refuges
Bayou Lacombe Centre
61389 Hwy. 434
Lacombe, LA 70445
(985) 882-2000
www.fws.gov/breton/
This refuge is home to the brown pelican and other birds.

Georgia Sea Turtle Center
214 Stable Road
Jekyll Island, GA 31527
(912) 635-4444
www.georgiaseaturtlecenter.org/about-us/
Visitors can see and learn about sea turtles at this recently opened center.

Important Words

booms (BOOMZ)—floating barriers used to keep oil from spreading

crustacean (krus-TAY-shun)—an animal belonging to the group that includes shrimps, lobsters, and crabs

current (KER-unt)—a movement of water in a certain direction

disperse (di-SPERS)—to cause to break up into smaller parts

ecosystems (EE-koh-siss-tuhmz)—communities of plants and animals and the environment they live in

endangered (en-DAYN-jurd)—in danger of dying out completely

evaporate (i-VAP-uh-rayt)—changes into a vapor or gas

flammable (FLA-muh-bul)—capable of being easily set on fire

friction (FRIK-shun)—the force that slows objects as they move against one another

oil rig (OYL RIG)—a platform and connected machinery used to drill for oil or natural gas

oil slick (OYL SLIK)—a layer of oil floating on the surface of water

phytoplankton (FI-tow-plank-tun)—tiny floating plants

plumes (PLOOMZ)—underwater clouds formed by oil

Index

Page numbers in **bold** indicate illustrations

About the Author

Peter Benoit is educated as a mathematician but has many other interests. He has taught and tutored high school and college students for many years, mostly in math and science. He also runs summer workshops for writers and students of literature. Mr. Benoit has also written more than 2,000 poems. His life has been one committed to learning. He lives in Greenwich, New York.